THE GENERATION OF LIFE:
IMAGERY, RITUAL, AND EXPERIENCES IN DEEP CAVES

Michael A. Susko

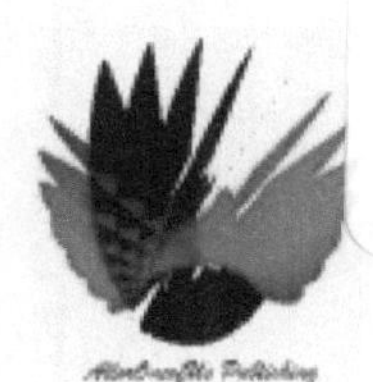

AllrOneofUs Publishing
Baltimore, Md & Huntsville, Al

While every precaution has been taken in the preparation of this book, the publisher assumes no responsibility for errors or omissions, or for damages resulting from the use of the information contained herein.

THE GENERATION OF LIFE: IMAGERY, RITUAL AND EXPERIENCES IN DEEP CAVES

First edition. August 11, 2021.

ISBN: 979-8201249885

Written by Michael A. Susko.

Table of Contents

To the Mayan people of the villages in Alta Verazpaz.

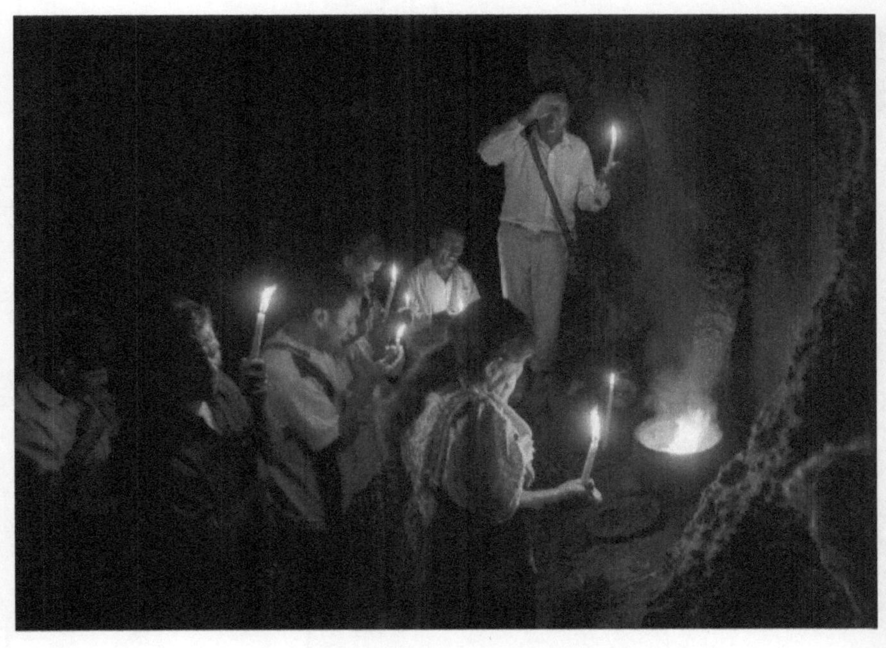

Mayan Thanksgiving Ritual, Alta Verapaz 8/20/2007 [1]

PREFACE

There is a mystery about how real life and our study can intersect. We can read about fantastic things that happen in history or literature, and we can have remarkable things happen in our lives. This work has such an intersection, in which I had a numinous experience in a deep cave in the interior of Guatemala––an experience that changed my life. I had taught many years before this on the topic of rock art around the world, as well as paleolithic deep cave art.

The combination of these two resonate to create the theme of this work. The basic theme is simple. The *generation of life* occurred in paleolithic cave settings, in which marking the cave's surface was combined with ritual activity. A hidden theme, laying beneath this, is the tension between finished imagery, and chaotic markings that abound in paleolithic caves. From the oscillation between the two, creativity and renewal emerges, in which a "dying" gives way to life-giving forces.

This paradigm can serve as a useful principle for our own contemporary psychology––our need to incorporate that which would fragment or dissolve us, and move us toward renewal and life-giving directions. That our seemingly distant ancestors can speak to us and inspire us is a remarkable testament to a human universality in time. We are now invited to explore our deep humanity's early struggle to generate life, and how much of it paradoxically occurred in the recesses of deep caves.

INTRODUCTION

In the vast swathe of prehistoric times, humanity imaged upon rocks in their landscape. They created a type of "iconosphere," a layer of art across the face of the earth. The roots of this imagery go back to tens of thousands of years before any urbanized civilization. Extensive pigment use has been documented in Africa's Wonderwork cave, as early as 900 thousand years ago (kya). The first preserved naturalistic art dates much later to 60 kya, from Apollo cave of Africa. Between 30 to 40 thousand years ago, rock art exploded across the world. While many of the images placed in open air have weathered and disappeared, we are still left with considerable imagery, especially from protected sites such as caves. This work seeks to yield light on the meaning of prehistoric imagery, by making use of scholarly research, reflections gained from teaching, and the author's own artistic sense.

We start by offering two images which point to the interesting and enigmatic nature of prehistoric art. Deep within a well at Lascaux, a bird-faced, tube-shaped man confronts a bison with lowered horns. Nearby, a rhinoceros is turned away, with six dots by its tail. At Lausell, in a nearby rock shelter, a woman with enlarged breasts and abdomen was incised on a stone slab. Her right hand holds up a bison horn, and her body was covered with red ochre, of which only traces remain. How do we begin to interpret this imagery from a period as distant as the paleolithic?

Admittedly, any attempt to decipher the meaning of prehistoric "art" is fraught with problems. Bendarik warns that scholarly interpretation, devoid of indigenous informants, is likely to be projection, where even experts "seem to be wrong much of the time."[2] Furthermore, European cave art, whose full-blown expression began about 30,000 years ago and continued for 20 thousand years, left no living tradition into historical times.

Modern study, however, would not leave us clueless. Hundreds of sites have been analyzed in statistical fashion, giving us a sense of the repertoire of imagery, and their locations which provide context. General themes can be garnered from indigenous cultures with a living tradition of rock art and who preform rituals in caves. In particular, indigenous people from Australia provide a living witness to rock art practices that go back into paleolithic times. There are also historical records from ancient cultures, which detail symbolism and ritual practices associated with caves. Last, contemporary persons have personal experiences in caves which provide yet another evidentiary source. In sum, objective study and a variety of ethnographic sources can inform us as with a range of potential meanings.

In the scholarly field, there is a tension between those who offer a single interpretative framework and those who favor a plurality of meanings. No doubt many specific meanings for prehistoric imagery can be given, but we focus on one broad, organizing principle out of which a plurality can emerge. We take the position that, in the most general sense, rituals and imagery found in deep caves are associated with the generation and renewal of life. Paradoxically, the cave, a generally dark and lifeless place, a negative space compared to the lit, vegetation-filled world above ground, is seen as generating life. This harkens back to Earnest Becker's basic principle that ritual is basically concerned with the generation of life.[3] It also appears in a fashion with the earliest hypothesis of the meaning of cave art, related to fertility brought about by the imagery, and so called "hunting magic. As we will see, this is but an intimation of the full complexity present.

Let us first consider the broader phenomenon of rock art, found across the world and in varied surroundings. It appears close to domestic spheres, along travel routes, or in near-inaccessible places. In North America's Great Basin, for example, rock art is frequently congruent with residential behavior and daily routines of the society.[4] On the other extreme, several rock art sites are found in remote, aesthetic, and even spectacular locations such as canyons or heights.[5] Uzbekistan petroglyphs, as a rule, are concentrated "in deep gorges at secured picturesque places."[6] Locations are not necessarily distinct from utilitarian concerns, as one site is near a prehistoric mine. In Austronesia, painted panels are "remarkable for their inaccessibility," which includes the high walls of sea cliffs.[7] Remoteness, which involves danger in making and viewing, suggests special meaning is at play.

Two more aspects of placement are critical to our understanding. Rock art is often found near water, especially running water. This includes caves where wall art is in chambers, which leads to further spaces which have water.[8] Second, rock art frequently populates places that are between different ecological zones, suggesting a role in mediating transition.

Although prehistoric rock art is distributed all over the world, this work will frequently reference the European paleolithic, as it presents the earliest and largest body of documented imagery. We also rely on imagery found in caves, as their preserving qualities make them ideal time capsules. In deep caves, deposits of pigments, wicks and flame holders, tools and bear skulls specially placed, suggest that imagery and ritual blended in these settings.

Before delving into the meaning of rock art imagery and its potential uses, let us consider the cave setting itself. The mouths of caves offered a protected living space, whether during the European paleolithic, where winter was dominated by glacial cold, or in the contemporary tropics where caves provide shelter from torrid rains and cold mountain nights. Animals have long used caves as protected spaces, from wintering bats to baboon troops who shelter at night.[9] The walls of Chauvet are heavily marked by bear claws, and their floors are littered with bear bones and pocked with hibernatory hollows. With a glacial maximum 22 to 18 thousand years ago in the heart of the European paleolithic,[10] caves were probably a necessity for human survival. According to Gilligan, in his research of cave use by ice age Australians, humans don't like to live in caves and prefer to live in the open, unless seeking protection from the cold.[11] Early humans, however, routinely used cave mouths as shelters, and ventured into the deeper recesses of caves for ritual use.

We hypothesize that the exploration into the deep cave, with its beauty and danger, had a significant impact on those who made the journey. The cave's unique environment included fantastical projections, tube-like passageways which unexpectedly narrow and expand, and utter darkness held at bay by oil lamps or torches––all of which presented an unusual, almost other-worldly environment.[12] In view of this, it is no surprise that anthropologists have interpreted dipping into the cave's dark, watery, "uterine" setting as associated with rituals of transformation and change. Put another way, the deep cave provided an archetypal, *liminal* space, halfway between light and darkness, living and dead, waking consciousness and the unconscious.[13] In this environment, the possibility for transformational experience is heightened.

Thus, we offer the hypothesis that deep caves were a setting for transformation and renewal, encouraging a type of death/rebirth experience. In the cave, the normal boundaries of self could more readily be broken, and novel states of consciousness emerge. Along these lines, Smith and White believe that much of rock art relates to encounters with the spirit world and invisible forces. Keeping in mind this overarching concept of caves as a setting for change and renewal, we will now review three broad categories of forms found in paleolithic caves.

CHAPTER I
CATEGORIES OF DEEP CAVE IMAGERY

Our first clue to the meaning of deep cave art comes from the earliest imagery found. Deep portions of caves appear to have been "colonized" or claimed by fluting shapes with fingers and hand prints. By the Gravettian era, caves were routinely graced with hand prints from all ages and sexes. Such prints may have been a sign that individuals or groups were present and that they had an important experience. The *act* of making impressions may have held special importance, in which the drawing hand was experienced as a conduit for power to flow.[14]

Beyond hand impresses, three broad categories of cave markings present: (1.) Figurative forms; (2.) Partial and/or indeterminate forms; and (3.) geometric or abstract signs.

1. Figurative Imagery

First, we consider imagery that obviously refers to the natural world. The dominant figurative image of the European paleolithic were *animals,* a fact so fundamental that it could be glossed over. Animals were vital to the existence of early humanity, providing food for sustenance, tools for daily living, and hides for clothing and shelter. This primacy of focus included making images, so we can infer that animals were not only good to hunt and process, but were good to image, to think about and reflect upon.

The hunt of animals and making their image could well be intertwined. When the Aranta from Australia were asked by ethnologist why they painted images of animals before hunting, they answered, "But how can we go hunting if we do not paint first?"[15]

Animals were also good to be merged with, for we find depictions of hybrid animal-humans. This is consistent with the fact that animals are of prime importance for indigenous cultures, and that they were integrated as *subjects*.[16] Many indigenous narratives offer themes that confirm this, including human-animal transformations, animals as spirit helpers who serve as conduits for sacred power, and marriages between humans and animals. An animal might also serve as a unifying symbol, or a "totem"––a sacral symbol that helped communities to rise above the competing needs of individuals.

Although the precise motive for making animal imagery and what a particular animal might mean remains speculative, suggestive evidence is becoming available. Recently, a hierarchy of animals has been found in paleolithic iconography, with the horse being primary. Their portrayals are the most numerous, widespread, and consistent in spanning the time horizon, such that they are described as "the pivot of iconography." This is seconded by the horse often being drawn much larger than neighboring animals, in an atypical right profile, and in locations that create a spectacular visual effect.[17] In short, the horse served as a type of organizing center, whether it be as a "totem," conduit to spiritual power, or whatever hypothesis we might offer.

Keeping in mind the animal's centrality, let us detail specific traits of how paleolithic people represented its imagery. The animals that dominant cave art, by their size and position, are typically drawn naturalistically, without a large degree of stylization or abstraction. Thus, animal imagery is immediately recognizable and accessible to us, and reflects the beauty of the natural world. That being said, animals were often drawn with varying degrees of disproportion and simplification.

Despite the naturalistic emphasis, there are clues that more is happening than simple representation. Imagery is often placed in areas that are difficult to access in the otherworldly setting of the deep cave. The animals are not drawn on a landscape line or with other identifying physical markers around them. The undulating water-formed interior of the cave creates the impression that the animals are hung in space, as if floating in another medium. Additionally, they are often drawn in an overlapping tapestry which appears to disregard earlier figures. Rather than a naturalistic group of animal grazing or hunting, we find a potpourri, a consortium of unusual animal groupings posed in every direction, scenes not typically found in nature. In short, groupings of animals are not a real-world composition.

Last, we note animal depictions make use of the cave's physical features. A hump in the stone may become part of an animal's back, or an animal may appear to be emerging or entering a crevice. This intertwining of image and surface heightens aesthetic appeal and suggests a realm behind the wall. Whitley takes these three factors to mean that paleolithic imagery has a spiritual role and is related to shamanistic practices.[18]

Another emphasis, more congruent with this work's theme, is that the spiritual role of imagery is related to birth, death and rebirth of animals. That is, forces of the deep earth are associated with generating animals as a place of birth, rather than an above-ground setting. Robert Lamblin's position concurs, when he describes the paleolithic painted cave as a "kind of womb-lair which generated animal fauna."[19]

We add a fourth factor pointing toward more complex meaning at play with largely naturalistic representations. Geometric signs were routinely paired with animals. The rhinoceroses at Chauvet, for example, were painted with a large, vertical band down their middle. Similarly, at Les Trois-Frerres, zigzag signs are commonly linked with bison. In a survey of 28 caves, Igarashi found that 60% of paleolithic signs were associated with figurative representations.[20] This supports the impression that animal figures were laden with additional meaning.

To summarize, we hypothesize that cave imagery is about generating life for paleolithic people. Before we go further, let us turn to a personal experience of the author in the deep interior of Guatemala, where indigenous people have preserved ancient rites. In a Mayan Thanksgiving ritual, called the *Mayajat*, the elders' prayers focused on thanks for the bounty of the natural world, from animals, which included insects, and plants such as maize which brought sustenance. There was also a petition for forgiveness for taking from the earth, a recognition of the cost in their taking. In a second part of the Mayajat, petitions are made for the blessings to continue, coupling the past with the future. In this cave, an ancient Mayan ritual site that also hosts a burial, there is a certitude that powerful spiritual forces being present and that petitions would be granted.

This example is confirming that rituals are found in deep caves related to bounty, which enables human survival. Paleolithic caves that held imagery were often near good hunting grounds, migration routes, or fishing sites in river valleys.[21] Similarly, Cos California's rock art, which is replete with shamanistic imagery and hunting scenes, were often found near hunting blinds.[22] Thus, a reasonable hypothesis can be offered that images and accompanying rituals were related to thanksgiving for animals, with the expectation that such blessings continue.

Envisioning "powers behind animals" illustrates how quickly this theme of fertility can become more complex when we consider indigenous formulations. For example, in circumpolar cultures, elaborate rituals were directed to a "Master of Animals," who served as a power which could recycle the souls of slain animals. In an ancient Georgian complex from the Caucuses, the hunter of animals was granted success because of his special love relationship with the "Mistress of Beasts," the supernatural owner of animals.[23] In ancient north Asian rock art, the repeated image of a birthing woman with a plethora of animals has been interpreted as a ritual invocation of "the female source of life" which replenished or recreated animal life.[24] The Inuit's shamanic spirit-helpers were ambivalent beings––young or old, representing the deceased or the spirit world, male or female. These mixed beings were also the *owners* of the animals, serving as conduits of plenty in granting hunters game, and bringing ecstatic experiences of light and joy.[25]

Keeping in mind the importance of hunting and its connection to the spirit world, let us return to paleolithic representations. Early in the Upper Paleolithic, during the Aurignacian era, 31 and 33 kya, Vogelherd cave was a site of food processing for horse and deer, and also for making figurative artwork of large mammals, personal ornaments, and tools. During the general paleolithic, Clottes states that cave artists "chose to represent the big herbivores which they hunted, especially horses."[26] So there is a connection between the hunted and which images are portrayed.

Not all is straightforward, however. Numerical proportions of animals drawn in a particular setting do not necessarily reflect the animals which were killed and eaten. Although the reindeer was a staple of the Magdalenian era, it generally made up only a minority of cave art. Not a single reindeer image was found in Lascaux caves, although remains of reindeer are predominant in the area.

Predatory animals, who were not hunted, were imaged. From the Chauvet Cave of the Aurignacian era, "impressive *non-hunted*" animals, included lion, mammoth, and rhinoceros––84% of the animal content. Likewise, early figurines from Swabia, dated to 40 kya, depict "fast, strong, dangerous animals": lions, mammoths, bears, horse, and large bovids. Other caves from this time period are consistent with this pattern.[27] In the late Upper Paleolithic, artists typically recessed images of predators toward the back of the cave. Thus, animal imagery in caves as being related to insuring food does not explain the presence of non-hunted animals. This opens the door that they were valued as a source of wonder and were associated with powerful spiritual forces, which would be life giving in a different way.

We note hunted animals could also be a considered a source of spiritual power. The San hunt the eland, which offers the gift of *nu'um*, or spiritual potency. In sum, hunted and non-hunted animals were dominant paleolithic concerns and the presence of both suggests that complex meanings were at play.

2. Partial and Indeterminate Shapes

No matter how often completed animal images are portrayed and given attention in books, much of paleolithic art are partial representations or have no definite figurative association. Although the well scene from Lascaux is well known, we are not typically made aware of the maze-like profusion of engravings in the rounded apse above the image. Up to half of drawings in caves have been described as *indeterminate*. Of these, the largest percentage are finger flutings, which have been referred to as "disorganized marks,"[28] which are not necessarily visually appealing, and which have often been historically ignored. Such meandering lines of adults, children and even infants who were held up, make for an "archaeology of intimacy" that focuses more on the process of making marks.[29] To sum up, a considerable body of paleolithic work cannot readily be categorized to a specific form and presents a maze-like confusion.

This impacts on the meaning of the dominant animal theme. Often, we find fragmented figures of animals: isolated heads, legs, and contour lines of neck and back. An animal might be represented by just its head, its cervical-dorsal line, or a curved, upside down, L-shape representing the animal's underside. Hisson goes so far as to say that the most common paleolithic theme is the *partial image,* in which there is a paleolithic preference for "broken contour lines" and "depleted" animal shapes.[30]

Why are there so many partial shapes? Are they drawings by young initiates or seasoned hunters, both of which came to make their mark in the cave? Does abstraction and simplification evoke the essence of things, an other-worldliness, or a spiritual dimension? Or do they reflect the reality of sightings, in which only a head or a neck and back lines are glimpsed in twilight, fog, or the natural camouflage of the landscape? Along these lines, Hodgson hypothesizes that cave art served as an "implicit priming," to train the hunter to see potential prey and predators.[31]

If partial shapes are numerous, there are a host of shapes which cannot be assigned to any definite form. Their meaning is obscure, and we wonder if they are simply unfinished works, playful experiments, or mistakes.[32] Perhaps some images relate to the processing of animals, which were disarticulated and used for food, tools and ornaments. The transformation of a living animal into sustenance, working tools for daily life, and ornament could have been an object for contemplation and imagery

We have given prominence to the theme that the use of caves is related to the birthing and generation of life. Along these lines, indeterminate or partial forms can be viewed as either *emerging from* or *dissolving into* primordial chaos or wholeness. Urbain refers to the "crypto-image, as oscillating between disclosure into an image and the temptation of the void to return to a non-image."[33] In a like manner, Focillon considers "a fissure through which we can introduce an uncertain realm, no longer extending in space or thought, a mass of images aspiring to be born."[34] In this context, it may be that full representations served to *control* that which is chaotic and wild.[35] To conclude, we envision a tension between indeterminate/partial forms and more completed forms, with a birthing/dying process in-between.

Let us return to partial shapes, forms which appear to lie between completed imagery and indeterminate shapes. Subjects may be half embedded or suggested by natural cave forms, and may seem to rise from a hollow or crack in the rock. For example, an artist from Altamira added an eye and a mouth to a projecting stone and created an eerie face or mask. A cave's surface may contribute to this sense of oscillation, as imagery goes in and out of view, depending on one's position and lighting. Because art in general employs such tools, Stone-Miller has defined art itself as "a perfect transitional state between." A dark and undulating cave space provides the perfect space for this trait of art, suggesting a dynamic interplay between realms. Thus, art forms found in caves lend themselves to a sense of birthing, entering from the other realm, or dying, leaving to another realm.

Forms in paleolithic caves have been interpreted as in a state of emergence from an inchoate group of meandering lines. Lorblant and Bahn document a host of finger markings on the ceiling of Perche Mal, which have on one side three women, one of which is superimposed on a mammoth, and an indented circle, interpreted as a "symbol of procreation." The authors reinforce the theme here, in which they describe "the emergence of shapes and figures out of an undifferentiated magma—–that is the birth of the organized world."[36]

This movement or oscillation between two dimensions, awaken tensions in human consciousness. World religions are sensitive to this. In Tibetan spirituality, transition states are referred to as *Bardo,* a continuous undulation between clarity and confusion. In terms of the paleolithic era, humans may have experienced the fear of being swallowed by the cave, falling into a primal chaos or nothingness. Along these lines, Mohen believes that the "swimming stags" at Lascaux, which appear to be partly submerged or emerging from inchoate rock, are reflective of the *fragility* of life.[37] In sum, half or partial images could well reflect existential anxieties found in the dynamic transition phases of in-between realms.

3. Abstract Signs

Between the spectrum of easily recognizable forms and indeterminate shapes, we can place discrete, repeated signs which are abstract and geometric in nature. Upper Paleolithic caves from Europe are graced with thousands of such signs, drawn independently or paired with figures. We find lines, circles, triangles, arrows and zigzag lines, and more complex shapes, such as rectangular tectiforms and wing-like shapes called claviforms. The regularity and complexity of some signs have led Keller to say that paleolithic peoples had an incipient understanding of geometry.[38] No doubt such signs were an important part of the paleolithic mind set, and perhaps a clue to their spirituality and the meaning of more formed imagery.

We could have considered geometric-like signs first, as they appeared well before any figurative representation. In a like way, children draw abstract images first, in which there is natural progression from scribbles and meanders to the figurative. Interestingly, children at two-and-a-half years exhibit an in-between, geometric stage which includes circles/ ovals, squares and rectangles, crosses and irregular, odd shapes.[39] The childhood comparison leads us to ask if the progression in paleolithic imagery is reflective of emerging consciousness.

Aside from suggesting specific symbolic meanings, signs give evidence for a paleolithic sense of syntax. One of the earliest attempts to identify a syntax came from Leroi-Gourhan, who hypothesized a duality between female/bison/circles and male/horse/arrows. More recently, Harrod has assigned four general meanings to paleolithic signs, with a verb-like action at heart.[40]

(1.) Circular and vulva designs related to life's potency. In terms of action, these have a meaning *Center!*--turning inward, or collecting inward toward a core essence.

(2.) Feathered or branching forms associated with birthing and growth. These have the meaning *Branch!*--leafing out, unfurling or unfolding, where energies are made manifest.

(3.) Arrows or double arrows signifying sacrifice and death, as hypothesized by Marshack. These have a verb like meaning of *Contact!*--splitting apart and bursting open, where there is a sacrifice to irrupting energies.

(4.) Wavy forms representing water and the flowing forces of life.[41] These have a meaning *Flow!* --pulse-flow, self-moving, an openness to the flow of life.

Thus, in terms of paleolithic art, a specific sign could be associated with the birthing of animals or the time of spring when animals are born. Another sign might refer to the animal as a generator of life. Or a sign might indicate the ritual of thanks in the aftermath of killing an animal. While speculative, such meanings are consistent with the basic impulse of ritual to generate life and meaning.

We add the word meaning at this point. For the sustenance of life is beyond just finding food to exist. Rather, human nature is such that it goes beyond existing and maintaining the body. Rather, we seek meaning beyond, suggested by our attention to a symbolic dimension. It is a basic religious impulse of humanity, for which there is ample evidence.

Let us return to signs which point to the generation of life and meaning. While specific associations are necessarily speculative, statistical evidence indicates a sense of underlying order. Along these lines, Sauvet has identified 12 classes of signs and a strict set of rules governing their spatial associations.[42] In a simpler system, Igarashi's survey of paleolithic caves details three general patterns:

(1.) The most numerously drawn figures are more often associated with signs.

(2.) Many signs are located on the flank of the animal, and

(3.) Signs tend to be either before or after the figurative representation, depending on its location in a cave.[43]

All of this suggests that specific meaning is at play, rather than a random placement.

Let us take a step back and consider that animals and signs are often paired. At Lascaux, the beautifully painted yellow "Chinese horse" with a swollen belly is paired with a feather-like design that recalls a branching/birthing association.[44] At Orne, horses and bison are like magnets, attracting signs which fill and surround the animals. Diverse shapes include hollowed cupules, flint inclusions, and patterns of fine engraved lines to finger flutings––demarcating a rich inner, haloed space in and around the animal.[45] Thus, animals can be marked with a single distinctive sign or a rich profusion.

The presence of numerous signs suggests an intensity and warrants further consideration. From a sheer biological point of view, lines, dashes, gouges, or markings could relate to bodily activities, including breath, blood, movement, sound, vomit, sperm, sweat, or excrement. Additionally, an abstract profusion could represent a life-force and linkage to the spiritual realm. In archaic Australian rock art, signs around animals are hypothesized to signal *marr*, or spiritually derived power.[46] Similarly, Smith hypothesizes that signs around paleolithic animal images represented a generalized life force, vitality, and a life-breath.[47] Interestingly, the oldest way that paintings were made and one commonly used was spitting paint, meaning than paleolithic people painted with their breath.[48]

Returning to the earlier expressed syntax, we find it consistent that the most common animals have the most signs, suggesting potency. The flank may suggest a localization or source of potency. The changing location of signs with regard to animals as one journeyed through the cave suggests that a narrative is at work.

Keeping in mind the general categories of shapes, and the most basic meanings, we consider a novel hypothesis, that signs play a role as an in-between indicator––that is, the *space in the middle*, between the oscillation of indeterminate shapes and more complete forms. We have already suggested that shapes are born out of the indeterminate. Along such lines, Boundas describes the intensity involved in the genesis of things, as "an ontology of forces waiting to take off."[49] Thus, signs may have played a special role in the transition or mediation between inchoate/fragmented shapes and more completed, holistic forms.

The placement of signs supports such a hypothesis. In paleolithic caves, Saintz has observed a general "concentration of abstract signs in hidden side-chambers" versus completed animal figures, more likely to be found in panels of greater visibility.[50] Likewise, geometric signs are usually found in the more restricted zones of caves in Central Australia, compared to figurative paintings in domestic areas, leading Morwood to say that the geometric represents a more potent sacred zone.[51] In East Timor, caves containing deep art have distinctive themes, including hand stencils, geometrics, and red figurative motifs.[52] Thus, we hypothesize the more abstract, geometric forms evoke more inaccessible and potent zones of power. In conclusion, signs are woven into the fabric of meaning of the cave with its imagery. Plausibly, *signs* are related to transitions, of which we now consider three.

CHAPTER II
BIRTHING

We have described the general context for cave art and ritual as one of a liminal space in which transformation occurs. We can envision at least three universal themes related to life's passages: birthing, dying, and transformation.

(1.) Biological birthing and psychic birthing. Images encompass pregnancy, the birthing of animals/humans, X-ray images of life within life, and abstract signs of emergent life. Related to birthing is psychic or "social birthing" events, such as an adolescent initiation into adulthood.

(2.) Wounding or dying, whether physically or psychologically. Evidence includes images of wounded humans and animals, fragmented forms, images scarred by projectiles, as well as passage itself into a cave. The wounded state may refer to a symbolic death experience, to the nadir or low point in a transition phase to more consciousness. This theme is more rare and problematic in interpretation.

(3.) Hybrid Beings: A variety of forms suggest hybrid beings: human-animal, human-spirit and/or an adult-child. The hybrid may portray novel being or end stage of a transition. A hybrid could represent a mythical being, or a person mimicking the being, who possesses and conveys spiritual power.

In this chapter we focus on biological birthing, which serves as the foundation for psychic rebirthing and transformational imagery. At the most obvious and biological level, birthing is the phenomenon of animals or humans generating new life or progeny. After the miraculous event of birth, early development follows: highly dynamic periods of change, where miraculous-like growth and transformation occur. A human infant transitions from complete helplessness and basic cries to an emerging independence and speech. Because of the high rate of miscarriage and infant mortality, early human development is obviously a highly vulnerable time. Thus, we can consider that early humans were aware of and highly concerned about such a significant and fragile process. In terms of life's later transitions of a more psychic nature, in which youth are born into the adult community, we can imagine that related imagery may have been used.

Before we examine specific imagery, we recall the cave setting where darkness, enclosure, and protection from the elements invoke a fetal-like passage and space. More immediately, caves may have served as a birthing space. Animals, from bears to canines, use caves as places of parturition, enabling survival through winter's cold. Indigenous peoples of various cultures often employed set-aside places and periods of seclusion for birthing. Typically, rituals insured that the mother and child are protected by providing adequate heat, proper diet, and time to bond with the child.[53] O'Donnell has hypothesized that caves and rock shelters served as ideal localities for birthing, as they met the requirement of thermal regulation.[54] In short, we consider it likely that caves served as birthing dens for early humanity.

Given the importance of birthing and the likely use of caves for such, we ask if paleolithic artists represented this phenomenon in their imagery or signs. In particular, we are on the alert for gravid female forms, bodies with x-ray views, birthing scenes, and fetal-like shapes. Due to the charged nature of the birthing event, we bear in mind that the mother and her birthing companions may have experienced alterations of consciousness.[55]

After this, we can ask if related imagery was used to symbolize psychic transitions found later in life. In this regard as well, women may have held an important role. Ross holds that females are more naturally able to access altered states, and that the first shamans were women.[56]

The experience of biological birthing and psychic transformation may have a stronger association than metaphor. In sum, our first theme concerns the generation of new life, whether it is actual newborns or the later birthing of a novel psychic stage.

Before turning to specific imagery, we consider further the cave bearing the symbolism of "womb mother" and birthing. The association of openings into the earth and female vulva are accentuated when red ocher is painted as if flowing from vulva shapes found in caves, and which is reminiscent of a menstrual flow. Many animal images of the Upper Paleolithic terminate at cracks and crevices, suggesting the association of emerging or birthing from a world behind the rock wall. Pieces of bones and flint have been found purposively deposited or wedged into cracks and crevices, pointing toward ritual. Such artifacts have been interpreted as fertilization by male shamans within the womb/cave.[57] In sum, paleolithic caves offers tantalizing clues related to fertility and birthing.

Indigenous examples can be summoned to illustrate the connection between cave and birthing. In a Mongolian initiation ritual, women crawl through the narrow passages of caves called *umai* or womb, where the sight of rock forms resembling a child or animal is a positive omen for birthing.[58] In Kosovo, a petroglyph with a vulva symbol, accompanied by asterisks and a newborn with a pentagram marking, is the site of a current ritual, a "passing through stones" to enhance fertility.[59] In an Australian paleolithic cave, *Koonalda* or a "funnel-squeeze" passageway has standing stones in zoomorphic and anthropomorphic shapes on either end, which is hypothesized to possess "womb and birthing (rebirth symbolism)." Interestingly, contemporary healing workshops may draw upon birthing symbolism, as when participants journey into a cave under the care of the "Bear Mother," so the person can retrieve their lost "fetus soul."[60]

The theme of cave as a womb and generator of life is a widespread association with roots in ancient history. The ancient Mesopotamian water god was enthroned in a subterranean palace, where his mother mixes his blood and clay, and the birth goddess "nips off the clay and fashions bodies." In Minoan Crete, caves were associated with the birthplace of gods, most notably Zeus, along with rituals of rebirth and regeneration.[61] Eileithyia, the Greek Goddess of childbirth, had her main cult site in a Cretan cave. On the Grecian mainland, caves were popular cultic sites for *nymphs*, nurses and protectors of children, and were linked to ecstatic states called nympholepsy.[62] In Rome, the Lupercalia was held in a cave where two young males were painted with the blood of sacrificed goats. Afterwards, the youths raced about the city of Rome and flogged women to awaken their fertility. Interestingly, a sacred cave was recently discovered beneath the remains of Augustus's palace, a 15-meter deep cavity with a richly decorated vault.[63] In sum, antiquity offers strong associations between birthing, fertility, and caves.

Rich cave symbolism has also been documented in the New World. In Mayan culture, caves were sources of rain and fertility, the entrance to the underworld, the home of gods and goddesses, and the place where afterbirths were buried. Tlaloc, his name meaning "Path Under the Earth or Long Cave," was the god of rain and fertility, and the recipient of child sacrifices. The earliest New World representation of emergence is from Guatemala and shows a maize God bringing tamales and a water gourd out of Flower Mountain, the Cave of Origin.[64] In the Moche Peruvian culture, anthropomorphic mountains and caves were seen as places of emergence/birth and the *origin* to which the dead return.[65] In a Huichol creation story, after a child sacrifice, the child emerges from a cave as Father Sun––myths which have recently been used to interpret the famous White Shaman mural from the Southwest.[66] In the North American plains, spirit beings were said to live in a "house of power" within the rock, over which drawings were made. Every spring the Thunderbird spirit was said to rise from a cave to bring rain and fertility to the land.[67] Archaeological evidence from caves of Archaic Eastern North America has been interpreted as rites for "world renewal, rain-calling/fertility, and rebalancing…"[68] Thus, an array of examples can readily be summoned to show a strong association between birth, fertility and caves in the New World.

Last, we turn to Australia, which has the longest continuous tradition of rock art. A common belief among the indigenous held that children emerge from water holes. An elder from the Gwion tribe describes this intriguing association, where *Wungud* is the life essence or energy in all things. "*When little babies are born, they soft as the jelly. It comes from there, from the wungud water. That's why it's painted up there in the caves.*"[69] Similarly, from Gonorong cave of NW Australia, where the Woddordda still practice rock art, it is believed that ancestor spirits left their imprints as paintings, laying down in caves when the world was still soft. They are the source of child-spirits, first given to the father in a dreaming, and then passed on to the mother.[70]

It is time to examine the paleolithic record to see if birthing imagery is present. At the onset we are handicapped by the fact that scholarly literature has paid relatively scant attention to symbolism related to infancy and birthing. In an article entitled "Birthing in Prehistory," O'Donnell admits that "this aspect of human negotiation" has not been central to archaeological research.[71] In the European paleolithic, it appears that only a single article by Duhard is devoted to reviewing imagery related to children and newborns. Nonetheless, sufficient evidence can be gleaned from mounting and varied sources from around the world to highlight this neglected theme.

Because of the largely hidden nature of pregnancy, we might expect that imagery directly related to the fetal-life stage would be rare and obscure. Yet, in almost any compendium of world rock art, we find suggestive X-ray pictures, or forms within forms.[72] Studies from specific regions of the world offer no shortage of examples. In the Tom River region of Siberia, rock art dated several thousand years ago portrays a female moose, which appears to be birthing a smaller moose.[73] Rock art from Mesolithic India, which often shows animals filled with abstract designs, also has portrayals of fully developed calves within buffalo cows, along with umbilical cords.[74] In a deep cave on the Upper Mississippi, a Native American depiction of a deer with a smaller deer drawn within is described by Boszhardt as "almost certainly representing fetal deer with pregnant does." From the American Plains, a whole genre has been labeled "composite forms," which has miniature anthropomorphic forms embedded within larger ones.[75] Forms within forms are so common in the American Southwest that they've been interpreted as a convention depicting fetal life.[76] In Australia, there is a plethora of X-ray art, which includes the rainbow serpent with egg-like forms within, and X-ray women in birthing postures which have been interpreted as harboring descendants within.[77] Thus, forms within forms are widespread in world rock art and suggest to many researchers the interpretation of incipient life.

Although not highlighted in studies, the European paleolithic presents us with suggestive X-ray like drawings and forms within forms. At Chauvet, a "strange bison with an equid body" has a fetal-like shape in its abdomen. In the Panel of the Great Black Cow at Lascaux, there's a smaller horse within the torso of a horse. In the same cave, a horse appears to emerge from the abdomen of another.

Fetal life might be represented among the plethora of abstract or geometric representations. In a rock shelter of Basse, two isolated kidney shapes look like twin embryos. In another paleolithic engraving, an abstract female figure has an egg shape visible in her abdomen. Simple blobs of red, circles, and *U-shaped* forms, commonly found in the paleolithic, might be an abstract representation for incipient life.

Although indirect, another indicator of fetal life is pregnancy. In the famous polychrome chamber of Lascaux, there's a swirl of animals, many of which are heavily laden, suggesting pregnancy. The enigmatic "unicorn" possesses an enlarged abdomen which almost touches the ground. The six ovals found within the unicorn's body could be representations of fetal life.

Some time ago, Leroi Gourhan found enlarged bellies to be so common that they composed a stylistic formula: "swollen bellies and small expressive heads." More recently, Cesar Saintz stated that Gravettian deformation consists of "heavy voluminous bodies, short legs, and oftentimes tiny heads."[78] Some scholars have suggested that bellies become swollen due to eating the rich spring grass, leading to stored winter fat. This does not exclude the possibility of pregnancy, and some abdomens appear to be enlarged beyond any fattening for winter.

Rotund female human figurines from the paleolithic have long been interpreted as representing pregnant states. Although paleolithic women were sculpted in varied shapes from slender to fuller gravid-appearing forms, the latter include a significant percentage. More generally, hand-sized female figurines, sculpted friezes and ba-reliefs often have sexual characteristics, in which breasts, abdomens and vulvas are emphasized, and heads and limbs are de-emphasized. Of some 70 figurines and ba-reliefs from the Gravettian era, an "overwhelmingly predominant" number emphasizes breasts, vulvas, expanded waists, and protruding buttocks.[79] Some female figurines exaggerate the shapes so much that they are reduced to an abstraction of bulges, suggestive of egg-like, fetal forms. One figurine, reduced to three egg-like bulges, could include swollen breasts due to an advanced state of pregnancy. We concur with Marshack's characterization of the vulva and gravid belly of female figurines as an image and symbol for the *portal* through which fetal life passes.[80]

The placement of female figurines suggests ritual and birthing. In paleolithic Siberia, figurines were found carefully buried in pits, and in one case the arrangement in a semicircle of pits suggested to researchers a "birthing house." At other sites where placement can be determined, figurines were found in pits or tucked away in the back of caves.[81] White and Bisson believe that female figurines played a role in birthing rituals, specifically to insure the safe passage of mother and child.[82]

More explicit imagery has been directly related to birthing. At the site of Avdeevo, Siberia, which has almost as many figurines as all other sites, several have been identified as representing birthing postures, as well as the terminal stages of pregnancy.[83] At Lausell, a sculpted relief of a female with upraised knees has been interpreted by Marshack as a birthing posture. In a careful analysis of paleolithic figurines from Grimaldi, Italy, Randall White cites evidence for dilation at birthing.[84] In another detailed analysis, Duhard finds imagery of newborns with large heads, post-birth fetal posture, cephalic bruises from birthing, and the remnants of an umbilical cord.[85] Last, Airvaux has deciphered a 14,000-year-old, maze-like engraved plaque from the French La Marche cave, finding the outlines of a woman and a baby with an adult-like head and umbilicus. Given our thesis, we are not surprised several researchers have found birthing directly depicted in the paleolithic.

The birthing theme may have also been represented by abstract signs. Perhaps the most attested symbol from the paleolithic is the *vulva*, whose basic portrayal is a triangle bisected by a line. The association of this shape with the vulva is consistent with its placement in naturalistic depictions of female torsos, such as the ba-relief frieze at Rock Aux Sorciers. The first iconographic creations of the paleolithic were *vulvas*, found on limestone blocks in rock shelters in Vezere region of France. Vialou believes these early depictions illustrate that art has its origins in the *body*, which "creates both meaning and a sense of the future."[86] The vulva form, as already intimated, may be directly related to birthing. A fetal form from Vienna, France, has been identified as emerging from a vulva shape. Mohen hypothesizes that vulva signs, especially frequent in caves around 15,000 BP, were a symbol for "rendering life to small human beings." Thus, a case can be made that the ubiquitous vulva sign was associated with birthing.

CHAPTER III
PSYCHIC REBIRTHING

A strong case can be made that images related to birthing, whether realistic or abstract, go beyond a biological meaning to the psychological and spiritual dimension. Mohen, for example, states that rituals of initiation accompanied vulva drawings and were the "equivalent of a birth." Slifer elaborates on the symbolism of the vulva, not only as a sacred manifestation of creative sexual power, but as the "magical portal of life having the power of both physical regeneration and spiritual transformation."[87] Walter Van Beek puts it this way: "the phenomenon of birth is in itself a powerful symbol that is used with great expressive force in other areas of life, such as death and initiation."[88] Thus, imagery related to the female and birthing may also be tied to psychic transition phases of a symbolic death and rebirthing.

1. Infancy and Spiritual Power

We explore the theme further by first noting the paradoxical indigenous association between infancy and spiritual power. In several cultural zones of the American West, there are tantalizing references to rock art being made by "water babies,"[89] dwarves, "rock babies," or a spirit that is "like a youth but shines like a light."[90] Other descriptions include supernatural beings with lots of hair and having "infantile human physical characteristics, whose crying ('like a baby') was sometimes heard." [91] In the Great Basin of the American West, the sight of small footprints is associated with "water babies," believed to be a sign of a powerful supernatural experience.[92] One explanation for the association between infant and spiritual power is the formula *baby=shaman/spiritual helper*, but this equation doesn't explain the choice of an infant as a symbol. Perhaps it reflects the belief that new life is strongly associated with supernatural power, as it lies closer to the source of things.

Dreams may have been an important way to access this primordial power. A small but important part of the ethnographic record states that images of spirits, which were painted on rocks, came from dreams.[93] For example, Yuman shamans gained their power by remembering a dream while in their *prenatal womb*, imagery which could later be activated during a vision quest. Instead of receiving a spirit helper, the shamans gained power by re-experiencing the creation of the world. The Creator's sacred house was found in a mountain, and the shaman's shadows were as "little boys" in the face of the deity. In gaining power, shamans also obtained a visual symbol of the pattern of creation.[94] The latter example illustrates the intriguing association between dreams, child-like states, and spiritual power.

This hypothesis can be extended to the paleolithic. Eshlemen describes the shaft of Lascaux as an "abaton, or earth-womb, for a magical initiation of incubatory sleep in the womb" in which prophetic dreams were received.[95]

The theme of accessing powers through a child-like state is also found in major world religions. In China the Taoist adept has been identified as an "infant-sage" or as "a child not yet born" who contemplates a descent into the Mother Tao to rebirth.[96] The Shigon form of Buddhism describes a *fetal Buddhahood* in which human gestation is a "privileged period of nirvanic experience."[97] In Christianity, the gospels declare those who become as a child will enter the kingdom of heaven, in a second, spiritual rebirthing. Contemporary psychology has documented the child's rich spirituality, finding "lodes of childhood spiritual experiences," in which children naturally invent ways to contact the sacred world, such as "tumbling backwards" into an alternate space.[98]

2. Wounding and Dying Experiences

If psychic regeneration or rebirthing is to occur, there has to be a "death." This experience occurs in altered mental states. One of these more commonly explored is *trance*, often practiced in indigenous cultures. Trance is not a quieting meditation, but an active, dynamic experience. One common and initial feeling is one of death, a breakup of usual identity. What follows is a more *totipotential* psychic state, in which feelings of expanded capacities emerge. A person during trance may experience alterations in light/imagery, sound, sense of time, and novel bodily feelings. These can include feelings of the intense joy of childhood, alteration of bodily form into an animal, travel through mediums (such as flight through air, water, and even rock), as well as feelings of purification and internal renewal. Whitley emphasis the neglected, fierce side to shamanic altered states such as pain, anxiety, grief, and terror, along with combative feelings and conquest of visionary demons.[99] In sum, the more permeable and vulnerable psychic state of trance brings a strong connection to emotional and spiritual realities.

Around the world indigenous people have used a variety of methods to induce trance, including rhythm, music, and dance.[100] In India, swinging turns the body into a "vibrating, shuddering entity," a vehicle for trance.[101] Losing balance and falling disrupts the normal sense of self, a "vertiginous play" which Tuzin describes as being associated with spirituality and the gods.[102]

In the Americas, "sacred psychotropics" were commonly used to induce trance, in what has been termed "enthogenesis," the search for the divine through a hallucinogenic state. In the Amazon, the "doctor" takes the medicine to travels to another world and bring back a healing song or design.[103] Dominican Republic rock art portrays inverted humans, suggestive of trance, which are paired with trees known to produce a hallucinogen. Using a hallucinogenic tea to initiate shamans, the

Huichol integrates a ritual death experience, visions, and a rock painting ritual.[104] In the classic Aztec world, a hallucinogenic mushroom was described as the flesh or fungus of the gods and associated with Xochipilli, the "Child-god" and patron of mushrooms which are called "little people" or "holy children."[105] Last, "magic plants" were used in eastern North American Woodlands––a potent form of tobacco, jimsonweed, black nightshade, and morning glory. Their function, based on historical accounts of ritual use, was to induce altered states, communicate with ancestors, purify the body to promote spiritual healing, and to cement community solidarity.[106]

Paleolithic cultures may have made use of psychoactive substances. Berlant associates the odd, domed-shaped caps/heads of some female figurines with mind-altering fungi, the "primordium" of an emerging mushroom.[107] In a 7,700-year-old neolithic cult room, poppy remains were found with a great mother figurine which possessed paleolithic features. Sacred traditions from the ancient world, such as the ritual use of drinks, such as soma from India and haoma from Iran, may hearken back to prehistoric practice.

Interestingly, oxygen deprivation has been recently hypothesized as a mode for entering an altered state in deep caves. Experimental methods have shown that torches in conditions that simulate decorated paleolithic caves can create hypoxia. This, in turn, stimulates dopamine release and the entrance into altered states. [108]

Contemporary persons have used non-drug ways to enter trance. Stress postures, taken from indigenous figurines, and coupled with rhythmic sound, have been used by the anthropologist, Felicitas Goodman, to help Westerners to enter trance.[109] The author himself took a workshop in such practices and can testify that they can serve as an entrance to altered states which changes bodily perceptions.

Beyond wounding and dying experiences, death is present in caves in the form of human burial. In the decorated cave of Cussac, several humans have been found interned in bear wallows.[110] A recent find has found human remains in a deep cave associated with parietal art.[111] When the first paleolithic burial was found in a deep cave, it was said to constitute a "huge problem."[112] Such finds, however, are not surprising if the cave harbored associations of death and rebirth. In indigenous cultures, the connection can be explicit. The Walbiri of Central Australia, for example, believe that ancestor spirits, who contact dreaming stones found in caves, will emerge reborn.[113]

There are indications that paleolithic burial drew upon the symbolism of birthing. In the Middle Paleolithic, where Neanderthal remains dominate European finds, most burials are found in a flexed, fetal-like position, evoking rebirth. In the Upper Paleolithic, human bones were often stained with red ochre, covered with ash and/or buried with artifacts and animal bones, as if to revitalize the spirit-body. Interestingly too, burials or ritual deposits of female figurines have many traits in common with human burial.[114] Lastly, we note that while early Homo sapiens more frequently used caves for burial, by the upper paleolithic burials were more commonly found in rock shelters and human habituation sites.[115]

Not unsurprisingly, dying and/or wounding are associated with birthing and renewal. In Karen Armstrong's *A Short History of Myth*, an openness to myth and the sacred knowledge is associated with initiatory ordeals.[116] Along these lines, we argue that wounds, whether physical or psychic, break up the normal sense of self and allow for symbolic and emotional forces to enter.

Various practices, which we have discussed, can be experienced as a type of dying. Trance involves a lowering of blood pressure and an accelerated heartbeat, similar to the emergency response to blood loss from wounds. Thus, the experience of trance may feel like wounding or death, as when the San from South Africa report the initial experience of trance as a strong boiling, and painful potency rising from their abdomens. The ingestion of hallucinogenic plants can cause varying degrees of "neuro-toxicity" and put the body into an emergency response. To this we add ordeals of fasting, seclusion, stationary stress postures, and prolonged dancing. Indigenous rites of passage routinely incorporate such ordeals. In the North American vision quests, aspirants journeyed to remote places to endure isolation and hunger, where they await tears, in hopes of encountering their spirit animal. Adolescent rituals abound with wounding rites which lead to "birthing" into the adult society. Various wounding and dying motifs have also been associated with religious specialists. Wiercinski links shamanic initiatory death to the visualization of a *perinatal memory*.[117] Ripinksy-Naxon describes the shamanic experience as *returning to the bone or skeletalization*, believing it to be "analogous to a return to the womb of primordial existence."[118]

The actual making of rock art, or subsequent contact with the art forms, may be seen as using "wounding" to generate life. In North America, women went to rock art sites, pounded and released potency from "baby rocks" in order to become fertile. In the Kimberly of Australia, the beating of images with boughs helped to "generate" more young water snakes. In Southern Australia, an informant reported that round cupules on boulders represent the wounds of an ancestral being, the pink cockatoo woman and that ritual pounding sends out fertilizing power to the animals.[119] Here, the action may be the critical feature rather than the image, and the rock dust may have been ingested to gain fertility.[120] In the Colorado plateau region, anthropomorphs with elongated spirit-like forms appear to have been attacked with great force by projectile points, interpreted as charging the images in a ritual renewal.[121] In paleolithic Europe, there's evidence that gong-stones––where pounding creates deep resonances––were repeatedly pounded, scraped or rubbed.[122] Added to the fact that art was often placed in zones of heightened resonance, sound was also an important factor to the location of paleolithic cave art and associated rituals.

3. Images of Transformation and Hybrid Beings

Altered states and trance have been used to explain the generation of rock art. Lewis-Williams has interpreted images and signs from South African rock art as related to trance, a theory he extends to the paleolithic. Likewise, Greer identifies phosphene-like signs and shamanic-like hybrid figures from the Central Montana region.[123] Keyser, in the Columbia Plateau, related questors to human figures with rayed arcs around their heads and outstretched, disproportionately large hands, while spirit beings are marked by extreme abstraction and stylization, as well as emanating zigzag "power" lines.[124] In the Crow Bear Song Dance, the power animal comes out as the dancer's canine tooth grows to the size of a bear's, and red paint is spewed from the dancer's mouths as they enter trance. This ritual has been related to the rock art in the area, including therianthropic images of bear-men.[125] In Melanesia, Wallis cites ethnographic evidence linking shamanism, rock art, trance postures, and unusually shaped anthropomorphs.[126]

However the state is achieved, paleolithic imagery of humans suggests transformation. The European Paleolithic presents many curious humanoid shapes, such as unnaturally elongated body and limbs. They make up no small proportion of the humans drawn, with about two-thirds portrayed as abstract, elongated, or ghostlike. We hypothesize that some of these depictions reflect a transition phase involved in a dying and rebirthing experience. Likewise, Eshleman hypothesizes that the elongated, abstract-looking, bird man of Lascaux represents the experience of "regenerative trance."[127]

If the cave were a place for psychic birthing and transformation, we would expect evidence that youth were present in caves. Child and adolescent footprints and hand prints have been found to grace the floors and walls of paleolithic caves, and to make up a significant percentage.[128] The host of smaller etched forms, that are the least noticed cave markings, are plausible imprints from initiates visiting the cave. Owens and Hayden believe that the evidence is clear that adolescents took part in cave rituals. From the ethnographic data from trans-egalitarian hunter-gathers, we can make the case that children were initiated into paleolithic secret societies.[129]

Supportive evidence comes from Southern Australia, where adult markings dominate more accessible regions of caves, and juvenile markings are unexpectedly found in deeper, more difficult areas to access. Flood believes these traditions date back to the Pleistocene, when tribal elders took children to remote places to be initiated by various physical ordeals.[130]

If the cave is a place of birthing and source of vital life energy, we might expect to see signs of novel being. In paleolithic drawing, we rarely see a human form from head to toe, but rather a hybrid form. Before examining specific imagery, let us reconsider the cave setting. The deep cave can be described as a *liminal space*, ripe for experiencing fluxes of identity and hybrid states. Endsjo hypothesizes that entry into a liminal space, such as with traveling to a remote region of the world, is equivalent to a ritual initiation, in which a person experiences a confusion of space, time, and identity. In such remote places, mythology often presents a landscape rich in hybrid beings.[131] Although Endsjo is referring to geographical extremes, which may have entrances to the underworld, we can extend his principle to deep caves.

Congruent with this, Bahn believes that prehistoric rock art imagery most likely reflects mythological associations, whose stories are largely lost to us today. However, he believes it's likely that chthonic earth deities were involved. Examples from the historical era abound such as the Greek Eleusian mysteries, where initiates entered an underground darkened chamber and offered piglets who had chthonic associations. Initiates participated in the suffering of the Goddess[132] and saw visions of her—perhaps Persephone's return from the underworld and the arrival of spring.

Paleolithic imagery suggests that caves served as settings for hybrid transformation. In many major caves, at least one outstanding animal-human hybrid appears, from the bird-man in the pit of Lascaux to the bright red mammoth-human from Chaos Hall of the distant Urals.[133] Such hybrids are typically located in more remote, hidden parts of the cave, whether it is chimneys, wells, or hanging rocks. As just intimated, such "end zones" may have been potent change-places, where ordinary reality is more readily turned upside down and supernatural powers become present.

We don't know if the hybrids represent mythological figures, feelings of transformations, or dreams, or if masked humans enacting a ritual. In the latter interpretation, animal-cloaked trancers wearing masks mimed animal behavior during intense rhythmic dance, in which they "become" the animal. Consistent with the theme of rebirthing, masks have been interpreted as indicating a period of transformation in which human identity becomes ambiguous.[134]

Although the most commonly recognized paleolithic hybrid is a mix of animal-human, there are suggestions that something more is at play.[135] At Combarelles, for example, a goose-like, semi-humanoid form has a half-bent, plump body with a long neck, round snoutish head and upraised hands.[136] Scholars debate how to categorize such forms and have created novel categories to describe them, such as biomorphs.

The pairing with abstracts signs also suggests more than a literal meaning is involved. From the earliest figurative painting period in

North America, a human top is paired with an abstract *circular* torso and several appendage-like projections three quarters of the way around.[137] Such enigmatic, part-naturalistic, part-geometric figures evoke a sense of otherness, and lead us to consider if hybrids have a spirit or dream connection.[138] In an example from South Africa, a recently discovered rock art panel portrays an abstract expanding spiral paired with a hybrid therianthrope.[139]

The hybrid's access to the spiritual domain may due to its connection to primordial times, when potency was present at the beginning. In the American Southwest, the Zuni "moss man" is imaged as half-human and half-lizard with primitive webbed hands and feet. Such unfinished beings were described as *raw*, connected with the potency of the first times, and more powerful than any "finished" human beings.[140]

If the hybrid state brought power, it also brought risks. Becoming an "animal" might go too far and submerge one into an animal state. In the mysteries at the shrine of the Lycaean Zeus in an Arcadian cave, participants could turn into wolves. In the literary genre, "skin changings" or transitions to hybrid states brought risks of psychic instability, madness, and death.[141]

We conclude this section by considering a newly found painting of a hybrid from Chauvet, one of the earliest painted paleolithic caves. A bison man is painted on a projection hanging from the roof, all of which looks curiously fetal like––armless and with tapering unformed legs. In the center of his torso is a black vulva design with a grooved slit, the classic female symbol. Thus, the figure is embedded in a larger image, which has been analyzed to be the lower half of a Venus female form.[142] To the left of this complex, there is an image of a lion. The themes we have discussed merge in a confluence: an animal-human hybrid embedded in a generative female form and paired with a dangerous

animal predator. We have come full circle, where birthing and the female
are linked to hybrid transformation.

SUMMARY AND CONCLUSION

This essay began with the liminal setting of the deep cave and the set-aside nature of rock art. In this context, paleolithic imagery was divided into three categories of form: 1.) The naturalistic animal, in which dangerous/impressive animals were a dominant theme. 2.) Partial or inchoate shapes, out of which more specific entities appear to have birthed, oscillated, and/or dissolved; 3.) More simplified, geometric signs, organized in a syntax, whose outlines we are beginning to discern.

In the second and third chapter, we considered imagery organized around the themes of 1.) Biological birthing. 2.) Psychic Birthing which invoked the spiritual power of infancy and childhood. Wounding caused by various means including injury, trance, psychotropics––all of which evoke birth-death symbolism, and 3.) Transformation to hybrid states which have a special connection to spiritual power and primordial times. These three themes concern passages which are universal in the human condition: birthing, wounding/dying, and transformation.

The main categories of paleolithic markings and the narrative themes are all related. We considered a dynamic tension between the figurative and more inchoate shapes and that this tension may have been mediated by geometric signs. In terms of narrative, we envisioned birthing/rebirthing scenarios, in which humans go through a chaotic, change state and have a renewal experience. The change process and/or the new state of being may be represented by hybrid forms, especially animal-humans in the age of the paleolithic.

To conclude, this work provides a scaffolding upon which we may consider paleolithic imagery. In the main, we relate the deep cave space and its imagery to transition-states that are basic to the human experience. All humans experience birthing, wounding and transformation to new states. Our study also serves as an invitation to become more conscious of these change states, liminal spaces, along with an invitation to make use of them. If paleolithic and indigenous cultures are any witnesses to human nature, it demonstrates the strong desire to be renewed and to be connected to powers beyond oneself.

In an indigenous cave ritual of the Mayan Thanksgiving, the author experienced a sense of dying and rebirthing. Upon entering the cave with barefoot Mayan elders, I felt the risk of entering the deepness and darkness of the deep cave, and a point of letting go of self, and thus "dying." During the intoned out loud period of petitions, I stopped from photographing and offered a silent petition to be more loving to my newly married wife. Then my normal boundaries of the self seemed to break down, and my consciousness became flooded with light and warmth. There arose within me a petition, for which I was not conscious before: "You will have a child." I sensed the petition would surely be granted. I also knew I must not tell about this until after it happened. A year and a half later, back in the states and a day after our Thanksgiving, two middle-aged parents had their only born child.

Ancient rituals in deep caves (or equivalent places for questing) may seem to be too removed, mysterious, and inexplicable. But the paradoxical meaning and beauty can be summed up in a simple phrase: the generation of new life.

ENDNOTES

[1] Image is also documented in *Haiku and Photos: Guatemalan Highlands*, (2020) Baltimore: AllrOneofUs Publishing.

[2]. Personal communication with Robert Bednarik, Email dated March 12, 2003.

[3]. Becker, E. 1973. The Denial of Death. Free Press, New York.

[4].Quinlan, A. & Woody, A. (2003). Marks of Distinction: Rock art and ethnic identification in the Great Basin. *American Antiquity*, 68(2): 372-390.

[5]. Clottes, J. (2002). *World Rock Art*. (p. 6)L. A. CA: The Getty Conservation Institute.

[6]. Khuzhanazarov, M. (1999). Ancient rock art in Uzbekistan. *Archaologische Mitteilungen Aus Iran and Turan*. Berlin: Dietrich Reimer Verlag.

[7]. O'Connor, S. (2003). Nine new painted rock art sites from East Timor in the context of the Western Pacific Region. *Asian Perspectives*, 42(1): 96-126

[8]. Bahn, P. (2010) *Prehistoric Rock Art* (p. 140). Cambridge: Cambridge University Press.

[9]. McGrew, W., McKee, J. Tutin, C. (2003). Primates in caves: Two new reports of Paio spp. *Journal in Human Evolution*, 44: 521-526.

[10]. Lewin, R. & Foley, R. (2004) *Principles of Human Evolution*. (p. 475) Oxford UK: Blackwell Publishing.

[11]. Quoted in "Ice age Australians sheltered in caves," September 24, 07, by Anna Salle ABC Science Online. http://www.abc.net.au/science/news/stories/2007/2039661.htm

[12]. Walthan, A. (1976). *The World of Caves*. London: Orbis Publishing House.

[13]. Devereux, P.(2000). The Sacred Place: The ancient origin of holy and mystical sites. (see page 87-96). London: Caseel & Co.

[14]. On March 7, 2004 the author dreamt while writing this essay that he moved his hand over a paper and the symbols magically appeared on a maze-like religious shrine.

[15] Clottes, J. (2012) Ritual Cave Use in European Paleolithic Caves. In (ed. Moyer H.) *Sacred Darkness: A Global Perspective on the Ritual Use of Caves.* Boulder: University Press of Colorado.

[16]. Lingis, A. (2001). Ecological consciousness. *Critical Horizons,* 2(1):

[17] Sauvet, G. (2019) The hierarchy of animals in the Paleolithic Iconography. *Journal of Archaeological Science:* Reports 28.

[18]. Whitley, D. (2009). *Cave Paintings and the Human Spirit: The Origin of Creativity and Belief.* Amherst NY: Prometheus Books.

[19]. Robert-Lamblin J. (2003). Other points of view - Chauvet: A New Chapter in the History of Art. In *Chauvet Cave: The Art of Earliest Times,* directed by Jean Clottes. University of Utah Press, Salt Lake City.

[20]. Igarashi, J. (2002). Relations between figurative representations and signs in three Magdalenian caves: Les Combarelles I, Rouffignac (Perigord, France) and Altxerri (Spanish Basque). *L' Anthropologie,* 106 (4): 491-523.

[21]. Beanune, S.(1995). Les Hommes au temps de Lascaux. (P. 204, 216) Hacherette, Paris.

[22]. Bahn, P. (2010) *Prehistoric Rock Art* (p. 109). Cambridge: Cambridge University Press.

[23]. Hunt, D. (2003). The Association of the lady and the unicorn and the hunting mythology of the Caucasus. *Folklore,* 114 75-90.

[24] Jacobson-Tepfer. 2015. *The Hunter, the Stag, and the Mother of Animals: Image, Monument, and Landscape in Ancient North Asia.* (p. 121). Oxford University Press.

[25]. Laugrand, F., Oosten, J., Trudel, F. (2002). Hunters, Owners, and Givers of Light: The turngait of South Baffin Island. *Arctic Anthropology,* 39(1&2): 27-50.

[26]. Clottes, J. (2001). Paleolithic Europe. (Ed. David Whitley) *Handbook of Rock Art Research,* New York: Altamira Press.

[27]. Clottes, J. (1996). Thematic changes in Upper Paleolithic Art: A view from the Grotte Chauvet. *Antiquity,* 70: 276-88.

[28] Lorblanchet, M. & Bahn, P. (2017). *The First Artists: In Search of the World's Oldest Art.* (p. 239). London: Thames and Hudson.

[29] Nowell, A. & Gelder, L. (2020.) Entanglements: the Role of Finger Flutings in the Study of the Lived Lives of Upper Paleolithic Peoples. *Journal of Archaeological Method and Theory* 27: 585-606.

[30]. Guy, E. (2003). Esthetique et prehistoire. *L'Homme,* 165: 283-290.

[31]. Hodgson, D. (2003). Seeing the 'Unseen': Fragmented cues and the implicit in Paleolithic art. *Cambridge Archeological Journal,* 13(1): 97-106.

[32]. Holl, A. (2002). Time, space and image making: Rock art from the Dhar Tichitt (Mauritania). *African Archaeological Review,* 19(2).

[33] Jean-Didier Urbain, (1991) La crypto-image ou le palimpseste iconique, *Eidos.* Tours: Universite Francois Rabelais: 5:1-16.

[34]. Gamboni, D. (2002). Editorial: Visual Ambiguity and interpetation (Quotes cited) *RES* 41: 5-15.

[35]. Wildgen, W. (2004). The Paleolithic origins of art, its dynamic and topological aspects and the transition to writing. In (eds. Bax, M. et al) *Semiotic Evolution and the Dynamics of Culture,* Peter Lang Publishing.

[36] Lorblanchet, M. & Bahn, P. (2017). *The First Artists: In Search of the World's Oldest Art.* (p. 239). London: Thames and Hudson.

[37]. Mohen, J. (2002). *Prehistoric Art: They Mythical Birth of Humanity.* Paris: Pierre Terrail.

[38]. Keller. O. (2001). Elements pour une prehistoire de la geometrie. *L'Anthroplogie,* 105: 327-349.

[39]. Hodgson, D. (2000). Art, perception and information processing: an evolutionary perspective. *Rock Art Research* 17: 3-34..

[40] Harrod. (2004; 1987). Deciphering Upper Paleolithic (European): Part 1/ The Basic Graphematics—Summary of Discovery Procedures. *Language Origins Society Annual Meeting* 1998.

[41]. Harrod, J. (1997). The Upper Paleolithic "Double Goddess": "Venus" figurines as sacred female transformation processes in the light of a decipherment of European Upper Paleolithic Language. In Joan Marier (ed). From the *Realm of the Ancestors: An Anthology in Honor of Marija Gimbutas.* p. 481-497. Manchester, CT: Knowledge, Ideas and Trends.

[42]. Sauvet, G. (1988). La Communication graphique paleolithique. *L'Anthropologie* 92, 3-15.

[43]. Igarashi, J. (2002). Relations between figurative representations and signs in three Magdalenian caves: Les Combarelles I, Rouffignac (Perigord, France) and Altxerri (Spanish Basque). *L' Anthropologie*, 106 (4): 491-523.

[44] Harrod. (2004; 1987). Deciphering Upper Paleolithic (European): Part 1/ The Basic Graphematics—Summary of Discovery Procedures. *Language Origins Society Annual Meeting* 1998.

[45]. Delluc, B. & Delluc, G. (1997). Les Gravures De La Grotte Ornee de Bara-bahau. (Le Bugue, Dordogne). *Gallia Prehistoire* 39, 109-150.

[46]. Chippindale, C. Et al. (2000). Visions of Dynamic Power. *Cambridge Archaeological Journal,* 10(1): 63-101.

[47] Smith, N. (1992). *An Analysis of Ice Age Art: Its Psychology and Belief System.* Peter Lang International Academic Publishers.

[48] Lorblanchet, M. & Bahn, P. (2017). *The First Artists: In Search of the World's Oldest Art.* (p. 231). London: Thames and Hudson.

[49]. Boundas, C. (2002). An Onotology of Intensities, *Epoche,* 7(1): 15-37.

[50]. Saintz, C. (2001) Main characteristics of Paleolithic cave art in SW Europe. *Muse Digital Archiving Frontiers*, www.muse.or.jp/spain/eng/caveart3.

[51]. Morwood, M. (2002). *Visions from the Past: The Archaeology of Australian Aboriginal Art*. (p. 116). Smithsonian Institution Press.

[52].O'Connor, S. (2003). Nine new painted rock art sites from East Timor in the context of the Western Pacific Region. *Asian Perspectives*, 42(1): 96-126.

[53]. Rice, P. (2000). Nyo dua hli––30 days confinement: traditions and changed childbearing beliefs and practice among Hmong women in Australia. *Midwivery*, 16(1): 22-34.

[54]. O'Donnell, E. (2004). Birthing in Prehistory. *Journal of Anthropological Archaeology*, 23: 163-171.

[55]. Personal communication with Laurie Rome, who has served as mid-wife, E-mail March 3, 2003.

[56]. Ross, M. (2001) Emerging trends in rock-art research: Hunter-gathering culture, land and landscape. *Antiquity*, 75; 543-8.

[57]. Clottes, J, & Lewis-Williams, D. (1996). *The Shamans of Prehistory: Trance and Magic of Prehistory*. (p. 83). New York: Henry N. Abrams, Inc. Publishers.

[58]. Humphrey, C.(1995). Chiefly and shamanistic landscapes in Mongolia. In eds. Hirsch E. and O'Hanlon M. *The Anthropology of Landscape*, Oxford, Clarendon Press.

[59] Krasniqi, S. (2021). The Image of tools and the metaphor for life: a case study in Kosovo. *Weapons and Tools In Rock Art: A World Perspective*. In Eds. Bettencourt, Ana, et al (p.63)

[60]. Proudfoot-Edgar, C. (2002). *Women, Bear Medicine and Shamanism*. www.shamanicvisions[1]. workshops/genbear.html

[61]. Preziosi, D. & Hitchcok, L. (1999). *Aegean Art and Architecture*. (p. 147-148) Oxford University Press.

---

1.   http://www.shamanicvisions

[62]. Larson, J. (2001). *Greek Nymphs: Myth, cult and Lore*. Oxford: Oxford University Press.

[63].Valsecchi, M. (2007). Sacred Cave of Rome's Founders Found, Scientists Say. *National Geographic News,* Nov. 7, 2007.

[64] Taube, K. (2021). At the Reed of Life. From *Flower Worlds: Religion, Aesthetics, and Ideology in Mesoamerica and the American Southwest,* Eds Mathiowetze, M & Turner. A. (p. 215.) Tucson: University of Arizona Press.

[65]. Hill, E. (1998). Death as a rite of passage: The iconography of the Moche burial theme. *Antiquity,* 72: 528-38.

[66] Boyd, C. (2016). *The White Shaman Mural: An enduring creation narrative in the rock art of the Low Pecos.* (p. 68) Austin Tx: University of Texas Press.

[67]. Keyser, J & Klassen, M. (2001). *Plains Indian Rock Art.* (p. 125) Seattle: University of Washington Press.

[68] Classen, C. (2015) *Beliefs and Rituals in Archaic Eastern North America: An Interpretive Guide.* (p. 176.) Tuscaloosa, Alabama. University of Alabama Press.

[69]. Doring, J. (2000). *Gwion Gwion: Secret and Sacred Pathways of the Ngarinyin Aboriginal People of Australia.* (p.236) Cologne, Germany: Konemann Verlagsgeslischaft

[70] Blundell, V. et al. (2018). Visiting Gonjorong's Cave. In (Eds. Bruno, D & McNiven, I.) *The Oxford Handbook of the Archaeology and Anthropology of Rock Art.* Oxford University Press.

[71]. O'Donnell, E. (2004). Birthing in Prehistory. *Journal of Anthropological Archaeology,* 23: 163-171.

[72]. Anati, E. (1995). *Il museo immaginario della preistoria;* Milano: Jaca Book SpA.

[73]. Martynov, A. I, Mar martynoV, A. Shimkin, E. (1991). *The Ancient Art of Northern Asia.* (Eds. Edith Shimkin & Demitri Shimkin). University of Illinois Press. (See Figure 28).

[74] Neumayer, E. (2013) *Prehistoric Rock Art of India.* (p. 127) Oxford: Oxford University Press.

[75]. Keyser, J. & Klassen, M. (2001). *Plains Indian Rock art.* (see p. 115). University of Washington Press.

[76]. Slifer, D. (2000). *Serpent and the Sacred Fire: Fertility Images in Southwest Rock Art.* (p. 59) Santa Fe: Museum of New Mexico Press

[77]. Personal Communication, Christopher Chippendale, e-mail dated 4/11/03.

[78]. Saintz, C. (2001).

[79]. Mussi, M. (2000) In Comments, The Venus Figurines. *Current Anthropology*, 41(4).

[80]. Marshak, A. (1996). In Comments. Self Representation in Upper Paleolithic Female Figurines. *Current Anthropology* 17:2.

[81]. Pettitt, P. (2002). When Burial Begins. *British Archeology*, 66: 9-13.

[82] White, R. & Bisson, M. (1998). Imagerie Feminine due Paelolithique, *Gallia Prehistorie*, 40, 95-132.

[83]. Gvozdover, M. D. (1989). The Typology of Female Figurines of the Kostenki Paleolithic Culture. *Soviet Anthropology and Archeology*, 27(4): 32–94.

[84]. White, R. & Bisson, M. (1998). Imagerie Feminine due Paelolithique, *Gallia Prehistorie*, 40, 95-132.

[85]. Duhard, (1993). Upper Paleolithic Figures as a reflection of human morphology and social organization. *Antiquity* 67: 254:83-92.

[86]. Vialou, D. (1998). *Prehistoric Art and Civilization.* (p. 55). New York: Harry N. Abrams Inc.

[87]. Slifer, D. (2000). *Serpent and the Sacred Fire: Fertility Images in Southwest Rock Art.* (p. 48) Santa Fe: Museum of New Mexico Press

[88]. Van Beek, W. (2001). Why a twin is not a child: Symbols in Kapsiki birth rituals. *Journal des Africanistes,* 72-1: 119-147.

[89]. Keyser, J & Klassen, M. (2001). (p. 122).

[90].Whitley, D. (2000). *The Art of the Shaman: Rock Art of California.* (p. 79). Salt Lake City: University of Utah Press.

[91].Whitley, D. (2000). (p. 90)

[92]. Pearson, J. (2002). *Shamanism and the Ancient Mind: A cognitive Approach to Archeology.* (p. 119) New York: Altamira Press.

[93]. Pearson, J. (2002). *Shamanism and the Ancient Mind: A cognitive Approach to Archeology.* (p. 86) New York: Altamira Press.

[94]. Whitley, D. (2000). (p. 92).

[95].Eshleman, C. (2003). *Juniper Fuse: Upper Paleolithic Imagination and the Construction of the Underworld* (p. 191). Middleton, Connecticut: Wesleyan University Press:

[96]. Tortchinov, E. (1997). The Doctrine of the Mysterious Female. In (ed, T. R. Soidla & S.I. Shapiro). *Everything is According to the Way: Voices of Russian Transpersonalism.* Brisbane, Australia: Bolda-Lok Publishing and Educational Enterprises.

[97]. Sanford, J. (1997). Wind, Waters, Stupas, Mandalas: Fetal Buddhahood in Singon. *Japanese Journal of Religious Studies.*, 24:1-2.

[98]. Pechowski, M. (2001). *Childhood Spirituality,* Transpersonal Psychology, 33(1): 1-15.

[99]. Whitley, D. (2009). *Cave Paintings and the Human Spirit: The Origin of Creativity and Belief.* (p. 188-194). Amherst NY: Prometheus Books.

[100]. Rouget, G. (1986). *Music and Trance.* University of Chicago Press.

[101]. Gell, A. (1980). The Gods at play: Vertigo and Possession in Muria religion. *Man*, 15(2): 219-48.

[102]. Tuzin, D. (2002). Art, ritual, and the crafting of illusion. *The Asia Pacific Journal of Anthropology*, 3(1): 1-23.

[103] Sullivan, L. (1988). *Incanchu's Drum: An Orientation to Meaning in South American Religion.* New York: MacMillan Publishing Company.

[104]. Ramirez. E. M. (Jan. Feb 2003). Delfina? or Devil's Herb. Ethnomedicine in Mesoamerica. In Hallucinogens in Pre-Hispanic Mexico (English Version). *Arqueologia Mexicana,* 59: 78-94.

[105]. Aguilar, M. (Jan. Feb 2003). Ethnomedicine in Mesoamerica. In Hallucinogens in Pre-Hispanic Mexico (English Version). *Arqueologia Mexicana,* 59: 78-94.

[106] Parker, K. & Simon M. (2018). Magic Plants and Mississippian Ritual. In Eds. Koldehoff, B & Pauketat, T. *Archaeology & Ancient Religion in the American Midcontinent.* (p. 119) Tuscaloosa, Alabama: University of Alabama Press.

[107]. Berlant, S. (1999). The prehistoric practice of personifying mushrooms. *Journal of Prehistoric Religion,* 8: 22-30.

[108] Kedar, Y., Kedar, G. & Barkai, R. (2021.) Hypoxia in Paleolithic decorated caves: the use of artificial light in deep caves reduces oxygen concentration and induces altered states of consciousness. *The Journal of Archaeology, Consciousness and Culture* 14 (2): 181-218.

[109]. Goodman, F. (1990). *Where the Spirits Ride the Wind: Trance Journeys and other Ecstatic Experiences.* Indiana University Press.

[110]. Aujoulat N. et al. (2002). La grotte ornee de Cussac, Le Buisson-de-Cadouin (Dordogne) *Bulletin Society Prehistore France* 99: 129-137.

[111]. Henry-Gameir, D. et al. (2007) New hominid remains associated with gravettian parietal art (Les Garennnes, Vilhonneur, France.) *Journal of Human Evolution,* 1-4.

[112]. Clottes, Jean (2002) Paleolithic Art in France. *Adherent.* (Extracts published at www.bradshawfoundations.com/clottes)

[113]. Morwood, M. (2002). *Visions from the Past: The Archaeology of Australian aboriginal Art.* (p. 225). Smithsonian Institution Press.

[114] Pettitt, P. *The Paleolithic Origins of Burial.* (See charts pp. 226-231). London & New York: Routledge.

[115] Pettitt, P. *The Paleolithic Origins of Burial.* (See charts pp. 82-91). London & New York: Routledge.

[116]. Armstrong, K. (2005). *A Short History of Myth.* (p. 34-35) Edinburgh: Canongate.

[117]. Wiercinski, A. (1989). On the origins of shamanism. In M. Hopewell and O.J. von Sadovszky (eds.). *Shamanism: Past and Present*: Budapest- Los Angeles (ISTOR Books).

[118]. Ripinksy-Naxon, M. (1993). Maya cosmovision and shamanistic symbolism. *Journal of Prehistoric Religion,* 7: 49-61.

[119]. Flood, J. (1997). *Rock Art of the Dreamtime: Images of Ancient Australia.* (p 146) Sydney: HarperCollins.

[120] Lenik, E. & Gibbs, N. (2021). *Rock Art in an indigenous landscape: From Atlantic Canada to Chesapeake Bay.* (p. 12) Tuscaloosa, Alabama: University of Alabama Press.

[121]. Cole, S. (1990). *Legacy on Stone: Rock Art of the Colorado Plateau and Four Corners Region.* Boulder, Colorado: Johnson Books.

[122]. Ouzman, S. (2001). Seeing is Deceiving: Rock art and the non-visual. *World Archaeology,* 33(2): 237-256.

[123]. Greer, M. And Greer, J. (2003). A test for shamanic trance in Central Montana Rock art. *Plains Anthropologist,* 48: 105-120.

[124]. Keyser, J. & Klassen, M. (2001). *Plains Indian Rock art.* (see p. 53). University of Washington Press.

[125]. Francis, J., Loendorf, L, (2002). *Ancient Visions: Petroglyphs and Pictographs of the Wind River and Bighorn Country, Wyoming and Montana,* p. 166 University of Utah Press.

[126]. Wallis, R. (2002). The Bwili or >Flying tricksters' of Malakula: A critical discussion of recent debates on rock art, ethnography and shamanisms. *Journal of the Royal Anthropological Institute,* 8: 735-760.

[127]. Eshleman, C. (2003). *Juniper Fuse: Upper Paleolithic Imagination and the Construction of the Underworld* (p. 191). Middleton, Connecticut: Wesleyan University Press:

[128]. Clottes, Jean, (1989). Le Magdalenian des Pyrenees. In *Le Magdalenien de Europe* (p. 281-360) ERAUL 1989,

[129]. Owens, D. & Hayden, B. (1997). Prehistoric rites of passage: A comparative study of transegalitarian Hunter-gatherers. *Journal of Anthropological Archaeology* 16(2): 121-161.

[130]. Flood, J. (1997). *Rock Art of the Dreamtime: Images of Ancient Australia.* (p. 93).Sydney: HarperCollins.

[131]. Endsjo, D. (2000). To lock up Eleusis: A question of liminal space. *Numen*, 47: 351-386.

[132]. Evans, N. (2002). Sanctuaries, Sacrifices, and the Eleusinian Mysteries. *Numen,* 49:227-253.

[133]. Poikalainen, V. (2001). Palaeolithic art from the Danube to Lake Baikal. *Folklore, Electronic Journal of Folklore* 18 & 19: 1-60.

[134]. Napier, A. (1986) *Masks, transformation, and paradox.* Berkeley: University of California Press.

[135]. Lorblanchet, M. (1989). From man to animal and sign in paleolithic art. In *Animals Into Art*, ED. Howard Murphy. London: Unwin Hyman.

[136]. Archambeau, M. (1991). Les figurations humaines parietales de la Grotte des Combarelles. *Gallia Prehistoire,* 33: 53-91.

[137]. Keyser, J & Klassen, M. (2001). (see p. 88)

[138]. Laugrand, F., Oosten, J., Trudel, F. (2002). Hunters, Owners, and Givers of Light: The turngait of South Baffin Island. *Arctic Anthropology,* 39 (1&2): 27-50.

[139]. See Painting from the NE Cape, web site www.primeorigins, co.za/rockart/ site of the month

[140]. Young, J. (1988). *Signs from the Ancestors: Zuni Cultural Symbolism and Perceptions of Rock Art.*(see pp. 121-129). Albuquerque: University of New Mexico Press.

[141]. Green, M. (2001). Cosmovision and Metaphor: Monsters and Shamans in Gallo-British Cult Expression. *European Journal of Archeology,* 4(2):203-232.

[142]. Robinson, J. (2003). Chauvet Venus: Latest News. www.bradshawfoundation.com/chauvet.

Did you love *The Generation of LIfe: Imagery, Ritual and Experiences in Deep Caves*? Then you should read *Mystery Stone from the Shenandoah*[2] by Michael A. Susko!

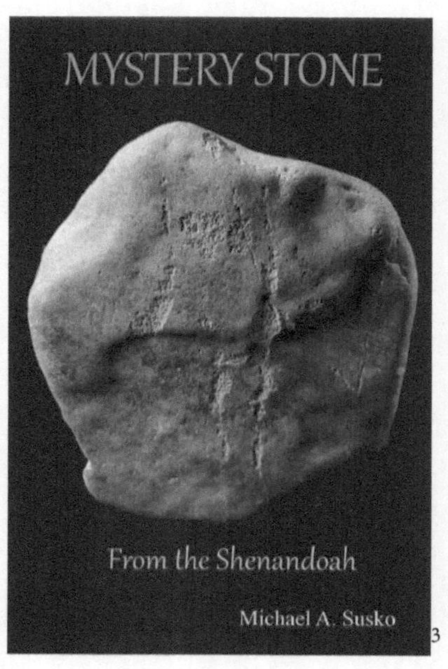

A beautiful tablet-like mystery stone has been found by the Shenandoah River, near Berryville, Virginia. Underneath its brown-orange patina, peck-marked shapes reveal a crystalline heartstone underneath and intriguing designs. Experts have differed as to how these designs were formed, so the author invites you to take a tour of the stone and make your own judgement. He illustrates the aesthetic nature of the designs and how they resonate with Eastern Woodland cosmology of early America. This includes the presence of a pervasive spiritual energy, the tension and complementariness of twins, and the archetypes of avian-man, earth mother, and skeletal shaman. The stone, with its images

---

2. https://books2read.com/u/b5XopA

3. https://books2read.com/u/b5XopA

supported by commentary, shows an alternative way to view the universe, and one that can enrich our lives.

Read more at https://www.allroneofus.com/.

Also by Michael A. Susko

Archetypal Worlds
Alwon in Another World: An Archetypal Voyage
Line On the Wall
The Alien's Gift
The Gold People
Spider Woman and the Timeroc
Quill Ears & the Other Earth
Darkwood and Dual with the Shadow Side
Giant Under the Mountain

Haikus and Photos
Flowers and Haikus
Haikus and Photos: Guatemalan Highlands
Haikus and Photos: Water Birds and Reflections
Haikus and Photos: Seasons of New River
Haikus and Photos: Yosemite Wilderness
Haikus and Photos: California Coast
Haikus and Photos: Canadian Rockies
Haikus and Photos: Hawaii's Exotic Landscapes
Haikus and Photos: Vienna, People with Buildings and Art
Haikus and Photos: Slovakian Castles and Hamlets
Haikus and Photos: Berlin, Light and Dark

In the Wild and Do One Wild Thing
On the Mountain and Two Are Missing
To the Beginning and Journey Through Here

Standalone
The Little People & the Time-Riding XiXiShang
Animal Spell: A Gospel Story With an Evolutionary Twist
Child of the Elements
The Firekeeper
Transformational Stories: Voices for True Healing in Mental Health
Caseness and Narrative: Contrasting Approaches to People
Psychiatrically Labelled
Ten Pulses of Evolution & the Surprising Nature of Evolutionary Time
Street Images
Transformative Experiences, Psychiatric Research, and Informed
Consent
Street Images II
Up Above and Down Below
Life's Dynamic Vulnerability: A Paradigm Shift in Biology
Alien Ally
The Generation of LIfe: Imagery, Ritual and Experiences in Deep Caves
Twelve Suspects
2084: Clash of the Cults
Bats in the Future
Guard of the Dead
The Imagination Being
Mystery Stone from the Shenandoah

Watch for more at https://www.allroneofus.com/.

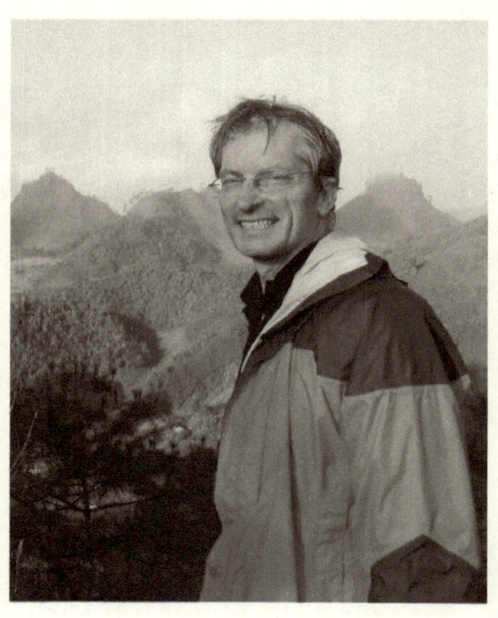

About the Author

The author, for many years, taught a course on "Sacred Art of Indigenous Cultures," and has lectured on the Paleolithic era. He has also made several trips to a remote Guatemalan village, where he experienced an ancient Mayan ritual in a deep cave. This work draws upon these his experiences and study in which he identifies a primordial pattern of birth and rebirth, which still has relevance for contemporary humans.

Read more at https://www.allroneofus.com/.